AIN'T GOTTA BE ...
...THE WAY IT'S ALWAYS BEEN

Why You Do What You Do
and
How to Do What You Really Want to Do

The Story – The Principles – The Tools

Written and illustrated by
Robert L.H. O'Connor

EyeSign Publishing
Springfield, Oregon

Dedication

To all my children and grandchildren—

Something to remember from Grampo.*

What is written here is advice, principles, and concepts

that I have wanted to share with each of you.

Some of what I have learned—by trial and error

(seems like mostly error),

personal experience, the experience of others,

inspiration, books, talks,

and just plain old thinking—is in this book.

Maybe there's a nugget somewhere in here for you.

See if you can find one or two.

I love you lots,

Dad / Pop / Grampo / Robert

*"Grampo" – short for Grandpa O'Connor
– The name is courtesy of some wonderful grandchildren.

Ain't Gotta Be the Way It's Always Been

Table of Contents

Give a man a fish, and you feed him for a day.

Teach a man to fish, and you feed him for a lifetime.

Chinese Proverb

Introduction

What are the primary motivators for addressing and maintaining personal or organizational growth? Two integral components of growth are knowing why we do what we do and establishing priorities based on values and beliefs. The process of growth also involves "decisionary leadership"—making value-based decisions with vision that leads to corresponding behavior.

Ain't Gotta Be the Way It's Always Been tells the story of a grandfather reaching out to develop a closer relationship with his son and grandson by taking them on a remote fishing trip to a little-known lake in the high country where the rare golden trout reside. Through a series of events, which include discovering the truth of an Indian legend, opportunities present themselves—where the grandfather has a chance to share and teach principles and concepts of growth as well as share some tools that impact a major career decision that faces his son. The adventure transforms their relationships and provides an opportunity for all of them to experience growth in their values, beliefs, and behaviors.

Ain't Gotta Be the Way It's Always Been is a story that illustrates the principles and concepts of decisionary leadership. Readers will be introduced to the *FIRE Principle*, the *Values-Beliefs Model*, and the *Priority Assistant*. These tools help set priorities, assist in growth and goal achievement, and overcome the strains and stresses of conflict.

Together, both ***Ain't Gotta Be the Way It's Always Been*** and the companion guide ***Decisionary Leadership: Tools for Growth*** will bring the reader to a sense of personal accountability in searching for and finding fulfillment and harmony. This will be accomplished with the realization of a personal vision and fulfilling objectives and goals by using the "Ain't Gotta Be" tools.

What is it that makes this all possible? The catalyst or key that unlocks the door to personal, corporate, and organizational freedom is the ability to set priorities based on one's core values and beliefs. With the "priority key," that door can be unlocked. So with this in mind, there is this simple truth: "It ain't gotta be the way it's always been."

Ain't Gotta Be the Way It's Always Been

Ain't Gotta Be. . .
The Story

Mountains, Lakes, and Goldens

The sun was rising over the small mountain lake; the emerald green and turquoise blue water was clear, clean, and pure. The breeze not up yet, the temperature cool. Wisps of clouds circled the tips of the three not-so-distant snow-capped, rugged peaks that seemed to scrape the sky. The morning star, Venus, still shone bright above them.

Within the ring of rocks, the embers left from the night before glowed brightly when blown on. With several dry twigs and more wood, the fire was burning again. Soon warmth penetrated the cool, crisp air. Comfort had found its home.

After quietly rummaging through the food portion of my pack, I found the bacon and pancake mix. A little while later, the sizzle and smell emanating from the pan set over the open fire found some senses willing to be awakened.

A head poked out of the top of a sleeping bag not far away. "Grandpa, where's Dad?" No tent for this one, though the sleeping bag would have to dry from the morning dew.

Seeing him sleeping out in the open under the wide-open, starlit sky was refreshing and brought back memories of similar experiences I had as a youth. "Your Dad's down by the lake. I think he's catchin' breakfast," I responded.

The head that had poked out of the sleeping bag had evolved into a sleepy-eyed, uncombed, skinny, thirteen-year-old. He wandered to the fire to get rid of the morning chill that had crept in overnight.

He and I had grown closer over the last year or so. His father had been traveling more than normal for work as a regional sales manager. I was available to go to some of the boy's soccer games and had enlisted him to work with me on some garden projects in the spring and early summer.

The morning sun, now bright and rising over the three peaks, shone down as the morning dew began to evaporate.

Looking down toward the lake to check on the fishing success, it was apparent that pancakes and bacon would be appreciated this morning. I waved my hat toward the lake, the sign that breakfast was about ready. It was acknowledged.

Today, our first full day, we would stay near camp and scout around to see what was here, explore a little, and catch fish. After all, we were calling this a "fishing trip."

Our vehicle, a green Jeep Grand Cherokee, was left at the trailhead some four-and-a-half miles behind us at the base of a ridge of mountains that rose nearly twelve hundred feet above our starting point. There were four large boulders that blocked the path of any vehicle going further. It was a long twenty-three miles of a dust, dirt, and gravel road we'd driven to get there. The trailhead was a small overgrown clearing identified by a Forest Service sign that needed some repair.

I had learned of this remote, little-known spot about a year and a half before from a friend whose car had broken down in a small, remote, country town. While waiting at the town's one garage for the car to be repaired, an old-timer had struck up a conversation with my friend and told an intriguing story.

As they sat in the waiting room, the old-timer shared the story of an Indian family that had been saved one winter by an eagle leading them to a mountain of gold. But the gold was never found, and the lake forgotten.

It had made an interesting story to tell a group of friends while sitting around a card table playing games one Friday night. For some reason, the story had stuck in my mind.

In doing some research to locate the place, I had initially come up empty handed. There was a reference on an old Forest Service map that showed an Emerald Lake at the location that had been described. Another lake, Lightning Lake, was nearby.

I called the Forest Service. After the third transfer, the voice on the other end of the line was able to at least verify that the lakes were still there. This Forest Service contact indicated that Lightning Lake had, at one time, been noted as a golden trout fishery but was now pretty much forgotten. She also noted that Emerald Lake had been called Thunder Lake by the Native Americans in the area. But about the time the local town was founded, it had been renamed Emerald Lake.

Feeling adventurous, I had thought to make an attempt to rediscover something—maybe some of the youth that I thought I'd lost—and try to bond and rebuild some family ties by bringing them with me to this area. What spurred me on was the nagging thought that had been planted in my brain connecting the Indian legend and the golden trout in the lake that had, perhaps, saved the Indian family from starvation. Maybe we could discover something together. My father had told me years ago that I was a dreamer. I had to agree with him.

While hiking the trails into the lakes near or above the timberline, our goal was to find the prized golden trout and take lots of pictures.

Golden trout originated as a native trout species in the South Fork of the Kern River in California and perhaps in one or two other Sierra Nevada streams or rivers close by. At least that is what is generally accepted as their origin. In time, some became hatchery raised, then planted in a number of alpine lakes of suitable environments. The Forest Service information about the golden trout seemed to be confirmed by some of the local residents we encountered in town—mostly from stories and hearsay—that Lightning Lake held goldens.

This was where we hoped to be able to hike to from our base camp at Emerald Lake.

Native golden trout are generally not very large. Most common are those six to nine inches in length in the higher elevations with an occasional fish in the double digits. Some of the hybrid hatchery varieties that have been transplanted outside the natural area can be quite large—up to several pounds. Native golden trout are a prize. Their color and beauty are second to none. Their head and upper back are an olive green, but below the lateral line, they are golden yellow, with a scarlet stripe along the middle of the sides and bright orange lower fins. Golden trout, at least in my opinion, are truly the most beautiful of freshwater fish.

This trip was the first real pack trip that I had taken since my son was just a boy. At the time, he was about the age of my grandson along with us now. My grandson, a strapping thirteen-year-old, smart as a whip and full of energy, had a head of hair that went every which direction. He had the athletic interests of both father and grandpa, but a body that had not quite caught up with his desires yet.

We had done family camps before, but none like this. I'd done a "pack it in and pack it out" backpack camp some thirty years ago. As a young man, I had camped in many remote areas, but as the years had passed, I camped less and less.

We had with us a GPS unit and had filled out the appropriate permits with the Forest Service prior to our arrival. All three of us had also taken the time to learn or relearn some of the cautions and precautions of making such a trip. We had each become first aid and CPR certified, and had completed several wilderness survival programs over the previous year.

I am about five-eleven, thin hair on top and gray, and was not in prime physical condition, being somewhat overweight. I liked to think I was able to get around and be active in some form or another. Recently, however, I had taken the opportunity to reinvest in my physical health, so I was somewhat better off than I had been for years. And that felt good!

Finding Peace and Meaning—Motivation

It seems to me that there is something about being in the outdoors that can expand a person's consciousness. Defenses seem to collapse, and if the outdoors are shared with others, bonding occurs, and, in our search to confirm what is really important in our lives, questions arise. Questions regarding family, career direction, or personal legacy are often pondered. What is most important? What is it that defines our character?

The beauty, tranquility, ruggedness, majesty, and power of nature can be our partner in that search as we seek to establish the internal compass that will put us on a course of success—to find personal worth and peace of conscience. A person might leave a place like this with the resolve to follow through with decisions made, knowing those decisions he or she makes are influenced by a higher source and are "the right thing to do."

There is a key that can unlock the door to successfully realize one's vision, hopes, dreams, and aspirations. That key has to do with setting priorities that reflect one's core values.

After unlocking the door, it is taking advantage of opportunities to make decisions and act on those priorities "with full purpose of heart" and belief that will swing the door open wide enough to find peace and meaning.

I had read about Viktor Frankl and his experiences in the concentration camps during World War II. His studies and writings found in *Man's Search for Meaning*[1] seemed to strike a chord with me as opposed to the Freudian mainstream explanations. I had also read and agreed with Stephen Covey's work about motivation and trust.[2]

It is my belief that as we exercise the gifts of freedom and liberty, our internal motives to feel important, needed, useful, and loved drive our behavior as members of the human family.

———————

While propping the fishing rod up against a nearby spruce tree, an audible sigh escaped from my son, the fisherman.

His son, the young teen, asked. "Hey, Dad! Did you catch anything?"

"Not a bite! These fish must be really finicky eaters!" was the rather slow response.

The fisherman seemed to have been preoccupied with something during the week or so leading up to making the journey here. Nothing was said; I didn't ask, and he didn't volunteer any explanation for being edgy. It had been almost like pulling teeth to get him to come the last few days. As our departure date approached, I had thought he would cancel, even after all our preparation. It was only after his young teenaged son reminded him of the promise he had made to come that the conflict appeared to have been resolved.

Pancakes and bacon filled empty stomachs. While basking in the surrounding landscape and sharing our wonder, the discussion took a turn.

A curious question from a young mind: "Grandpa, you told me something when you were at one of my ball games, about if I can figure out why I do what I do, then I can accomplish anything I really want to. I don't get it. How can I figure out why I do stuff?"

Looking back at the young man and nodding toward his father, the words slipped out, "Well, maybe you should ask your Dad."

There was a long pause. I knew what was coming next but held my tongue. The question was asked...and the response was as I had anticipated: the boy's father shrugged his shoulders, eyes focused on the dry dirt. "I'm just on my way down to the lake. Maybe we can talk about it a little later," was his quiet response.

Building Foundations—
Trust and Four Core Principles

As long as I can remember, he tended to avoid situations like this. I hoped that he would take a minute to talk, but he is always in motion—things to do and places to be— even up here in this pristine setting. I knew these were excuses. I also knew there was a reason for this restlessness, but I was afraid to ask—afraid if I said anything I might feel the pain of rejection if he didn't like what I had to say, fear that my fatherly love would be unwelcome to someone I held dear. This I knew was due to some of the unfortunate family circumstances that had occurred when he, his brothers, and his sisters were young. His mother and I had divorced, and that had taken a toll on everyone. Both of us had remarried within a few years. I love my kids. I have longed for a close relationship with them. Unfortunately, family dynamics change when the characters shift to a different stage or take on different roles and others come on the scene to play additional parts in the lives that are seeking to be formed and shaped for the future. Most often, stability is lost and is very difficult to regain except with diligence, patience, and work. This is an evolving experience that seems to ebb and flow with the tides of time and influences.

I long for the anchor of trust, and this is something that cannot be rushed or pushed—only earned. I have tried to be consistent and constant in what I stand for and what I believe. Trust is the anchor in not only family and personal relationships but also the business and corporate world. I do know this: trust is the fundamental building block of any relationship and the keystone in personal or organizational fulfillment.

Earning trust and keeping it is critical to some of our basic human needs. There are times in a person's life when trust might be held back because of personal perceptions and the influence of experiences—founded or unfounded, positive or negative. I know what that feels like from both ends of the spectrum—having been trustworthy, losing trust, and having to earn back what was lost—losing trust in someone because of their behavior and hoping they would earn it back.

Stephen Covey quoted his son, "There is nothing as fast as the speed of trust. It is faster than anything you can think about. When trust is present, mistakes are forgiven and forgotten. Trust is the glue of life. It is the glue that holds organizations, cultures and relationships together."[3]

There are times when I feel I have missed the mark and should have done things differently. And there are times when I hoped I had not sabotaged someone's trust in me.

I am reminded of some counsel I once received: "Where there is no hope, there is no reward, and the feelings of charity and love will dwindle and die." So I have learned to keep trying to develop trust, to have faith and not give up hope. By working at this in faith and maintaining hope, I have come to experience moments of sweetness, the fruition, on occasion, when trust is offered again and love abounds.

Faith, hope, charity, and love, or sincerity, built on a foundation of trust are the genuine motivating factors to succeed in building any relationship and to experience the joys of fulfillment and harmony.

All of my children are grown, and several have families of their own now. Over the years, from childhood to adulthood, most of them have experienced the cause and effects of unplanned change, such as job loss, divorce, injury, and health crisis, among others. Though these have been difficult passages, time has had a maturing effect on them. It takes patience to allow the course of change and growth to occur, and it takes patience to realize it may not be on a planned timetable. Truth and principles that are true have a way of manifesting themselves, but we must be prepared to recognize truth and act on the opportunities that are presented to us regardless of the difficulty. This is "conscience responsibility"—each person being personally accountable and responsible to himself.

The thirteen-year-old mop top turned toward me and laughed, "Earth to Grandpa."

I raised my hand and motioned him over toward the fire with a chuckle.

Among the three of us, we had decided to take turns helping to clean up and take care of camp chores. I had accepted the fact that most likely I would be assisting on all the cleanup committees for this trip. What determined which one of us would take first chore duty would be the winner of rock, paper, scissors. The young boy won.

I somewhat ignored his question about why we do things—but intentionally. I have learned it's easier to start talking when you're doing something together; I don't know why. It's just easier to ask a question, answer a question, or offer some counsel while working side by side. There are times, though, when I think I know what to say, but it just won't come out. That's when I kick myself. I've learned that even if what I have to say doesn't flow smoothly, it doesn't have to be perfect. The intent is what's perfect.

Grabbing the scrub pad, I said, "Let's clean up here and then why don't you walk with me down to where the creek empties into the lake. I think your Dad is on his way down there to catch lunch."

The FIRE Principle

"But, Grandpa, how can I figure out how to do stuff and why I do things? And how can I know what to do to figure things out?" the youngster persisted.

"Let's tackle how to figure things out first, I said.

I poked at the fire, turning toward the rustling sounds of a fishing pole being picked up and boots breaking through some brush on the way down to the lake.

I looked up, asked the boy still standing in the camp area to bring a few pieces of firewood over to the fire, and then asked, "So who taught you how to build a fire?"

"My Dad did," he said.

I began sharing my thoughts, "I'll tell you the same thing I told your father years ago: Look at this fire. Before it was warming you, it was just some wood, and then we used a match to get it started. But you can't just try to light the wood. There is some preparation that needs to be done, and you need to know what works best to get the fire going."

My young student interjects, "Yeah, Dad told me the same thing when he taught me."

I continued, "So tell me, what is most important in building a fire?"

With a pondering look on his face, he explains, "You start with little dry sticks or twigs; then add more wood and bigger sticks until the fire is big enough to put logs on it. Then you add the logs so it will keep burning. And you need to have all your wood by the fire before you start the fire."

After a pause, I said in a rhetorical way, "There is an order or process to follow, and it is important to have a fire-building plan, right? So let's see if we can come up with a way to remember some things and also answer your question—the one about figuring things out."

Picking up a small dry stick and peeling the bark, I caught his eye. "To get things done and have a plan, there are four things to do: One, focus on what you want; two, get information about it; three, identify and discover what resources you have; and four, engage in an action plan."

As I put the stick into the fire, a thought occurred to me that I shared out loud, "We can call it the FIRE Principle. F—FOCUS on the objective or end result. That means create a "vision" of what you really want or want to do. Like build a fire."

Wanting to become part of the learning process, the boy tossed a stick that he had picked up into the fire and asked, "What's the second?"

Encouraged, I continued. "The letter I—get and use INFORMATION. That one means to learn about what it is you want to do. You might have to study and ask questions.

"The third, R—know your RESOURCES. This one is overlooked a lot of the time. Resources are all the things that can help you. Sometimes our resources can be part of the information process. Sometimes resources might be something tangible like a tool—a hatchet, or matches, or a person like your Dad to show you. Resources are everything you need that will help to accomplish your objective.

"And the 'E'? ENGAGE in an action plan. Do something! So now we have a way to remember what to do! F-I-R-E."

"Grandpa, that's pretty funny!"

"What do you mean?" I asked.

"Dad told me once to build a fire under my rear and get down the soccer field! I needed to focus on getting down the field. He gave me information about why I needed to get down the field so I would be in position to help my teammates. My resources are my legs, teammates, and the coach, and I needed to actually run and do it—that would be engaging in action. I *was* able to be in position to pass the ball to my teammate who kicked the winning goal. We won!"

He pumped his fist in the air in celebration of the victory.

Smiling at his response, I reinforced the moment. "You're getting it! Humm…that's making me think—

back to our F-I-R-E. Here is a key: The match that starts the fire burning could be the reason you want the fire in the first place. You just won't have the fire unless there is something to start the fire with—that's the match. You have all the elements of good fire building. You have to have the small dry tinder—kindling and twigs that help the larger sticks start. That will help or influence the logs to keep burning a long, long time. It won't really get started until you strike the match and light the tinder though."

Purpose and Reason

"So what's the match represent?" the young teen asked.

"There is a major piece to the success of the FIRE Principle, and you said it a minute ago," I said. "Now what are we going to do with the fire you are going to build? Why have a fire?"

With a sort of giggle he said, "To cook the fish Dad didn't catch…to cook breakfast."

Continuing the question, I asked, "But what if you aren't hungry right then or you are just too impatient to cook and want to go catch fish more than you want a fire?"

Again a giggle and laugh, "Then I won't build a fire!"

His smile turned serious as I explained, "The 'why' is our motivation to do something. That's what causes us to want to start or act. So the reason that is most important, your top priority, is usually why you do something. Why did you run down the field when you were playing soccer?"

The young star pumps his fist in the air again and with excitement says, "To win! And we won!"

Does that help to answer your question?" I asked.

With a thoughtful look, and turning away from the fire and more toward me, he said, "Sort of. But sometimes I might want to do something, but it just doesn't get done."

Again I ask a question to help direct his thoughts. "So why else would someone build a fire?"

"Grandpa, you know, to get warm, cook food, and maybe we need to boil some water for hot chocolate and to do the dishes."

"Now that is getting more specific!" I said with some enthusiasm. "You told me something you learned in school about water. What have you learned about boiling water?"

He loves science so this kept his interest as he became the teacher. "In my science class, we learned that to boil water, you get it hot. We put the pot of water on the fire, and the hotter the fire, the hotter the water gets until it gets to a certain temperature and then it boils. When the water really gets boiling, then it turns to steam."

"Very good," I responded. "The fire, or heat, influences the water to boil and eventually to turn to steam. Steam can power a train, open a sealed envelope, and a lot of other things." Picking up a few more sticks to put on the fire, I explained, "Fine-tuning and determining a specific 'why' or purpose will help us determine how hot and how long we need the fire to burn. That would be the urgency, motivation, and intensity of the 'E'—the 'engage' part of the FIRE Principle.

"The more you want something or the higher its priority, the more energy will be put into making it happen.

Right now we need hot water for some hot chocolate and to clean the frying pan.

"So the moral of this story is to strike the match to light a fire and get moving. But if you don't really know why you're lighting the fire in the first place, you might just waste a lot of wood, maybe get burned—in more ways than one— and waste a lot of time."

We stopped for a few moments to get the hot water off the fire, find the soap, and collect the dishes. It took only a couple of minutes and we were finished, ready to dowse the fire, find the creek, then fish!

Our camp was just a few minutes from the small clear creek that tumbled from a snow field above and made its way down through some evergreens and aspens, past our camp, and into the clear emerald green and blue lake below.

I grabbed my camera. The mop top got his pole and ran over to the gurgling creek.

Think Like a Fish and Fish Where the Fish Are

Seeing he was engaged at the stream, I took some pictures of our camp and made my way toward the water.

A small Super-Duper lure dropped into some riffles and a pool below without success. Pointing my camera back toward the camp, I took another picture and then turning back toward the creek, I saw the young fisherman peering into the water.

"Do you see any fish?" I asked.

"No."

"But they are in there," I told him.

"How do you know, Grandpa?"

Lowering my camera, I conceded, "Well, I guess I don't really know for sure, but I have a pretty good idea they are there. We most likely scared them when we came over and looked in, but I think we might be able to put what we just learned into practice. Let's figure out how to catch some fish."

"Grandpa, I'm sort of tired of school right now. I just want to catch some fish."

"That's what I'm trying to help you do—catch some fish!"

"So if you were a fish in this stream, what do you think you'd be trying to do? What do you think a fish might think is most important?"

"I don't know," he responded sarcastically. "I suppose the fish would be trying to stay alive, so maybe stay in the water and find food?"

"Yep, food and water are probably most important—and what else?"

"A place to hide and be safe."

"There are some very basic priorities for all animals—and people. And these are what you just mentioned: food, water, and shelter. For now, let's use our FIRE Principle to figure out how to catch some fish.

"Remember the first one: Focus on the objective. What's the second? Use information. The third is know your resources. And the 'E'"?

"Be engaged in action!" the boy responded.

"So what are we going to focus on?" I asked.

"Catching fish!"

"What information do we have about fish? And what are your resources?"

"I like to catch fish. I know a little bit but not a lot about fish. They bite on lures and spinners and sometimes bait. I cast into the water and hope a fish takes what I've got. And if he doesn't, then I put on something else. I don't really know how to fly fish yet like Dad."

"So, a fishing pole, bait, lures—those are resources. A resource also might be used to help you get more information or better information. Let's use a resource to get information—that would be me."

"OK, Grandpa, so tell me where to cast and what to use for bait!"

"Do you see that large rock over there? The one with the tree branch beside it and the big tree just behind it? Look at the water. Describe what you see."

He looked in the direction of the branch and rock and then said, "Well, the water is moving fast around the rock, and it is slow right behind the rock. There's a branch partially underwater."

"I think there might be a fish right there," I said.

"Why?" the young fisherman asks.

Looking back at me with fishing rod ready to cast, he stopped and continued, "I need to figure that out. I haven't been very successful, yet."

"Your Dad and I were talking about this a while back, and we concluded that it's important to fish where the fish are. Think like a fish—specifically like a trout. Imagine you are a trout. You need to have a place to hide. You need to eat and have good water to swim in as well as a place to rest. Where can a trout get all of these the easiest?"

Pointing to where the rock and the branch are, he responded, "Because the stream gets narrow right there and brings food right by that spot. The fish can hide and rest right by the log and then swim out into the current, get its food, and swim right back."

"You're getting it. And what are their habits and preferences? Now you just need some information about what food is available and what food the fish prefers to eat."

"Grandpa, you are about the only resource I have. What do you think?"

"Why don't you get down there by the water and see what you can see? Look on and under the rocks in the water."

"Hey! I see these little small green bugs swimming around. And I saw a grasshopper when I first stepped by the rocks. On the rocks underwater I also saw these little bugs that are inside a rock like a cocoon."

"Well, I'd say you've done some good work. Good job! Now, to more resources: we just have to match up a fly or something that looks like what you have just seen. Or use one of the bugs for bait. The line or leader you use to tie on a hook is also an important resource."

I pulled out of my pocket a small spool of one-and-a-half-pound test leader material and tossed it to him with a warning, "Now, just be sure I get this back."

As an afterthought, I followed with, "By the way, there are some things in every life that are really important, like food, shelter, safety, among other things. We are constantly figuring out what is most important. That's what we call setting priorities. And priorities influence what we do and how we act.

"Not only is it important and helpful to know your own priorities and what you value but also the priorities of who you work with, your friends, and your competition. People are like fish; you will come across a lot of them out in the world as you swim through your life. If you know their habits, preferences, and priorities, you can determine your own direction and influence as it relates to them. Sometimes that might take some effort and patience, but it's a good thing to learn to do."

"So that's why there should be a fish right there. And if a fish is hungry and you do the 'E' part—engage in action—give him something that looks good with a hook in it—there's a pretty good chance we'll have fish for lunch. Does that make sense?"

"Yeah" is the response with that youthful animation in his voice.

"Now when it gets close to lunch time, go get your Dad and bring him up here by that rock and log. But no fishing here until lunchtime. We'll let the fish settle down. I think we scared them with all our talking and poking around. Let's go see how your Dad's doing."

The fishing bug had bitten, and the youngster ran off, scampering over rocks and logs to meet up with his father near where the creek emptied into the lake. The youngster was eager to wet a line and catch some fish. I was eager to take some more pictures.

A short distance up from a log jutting out into the lake, I heard, "It doesn't look like the fish are biting right now." Father and son began moving around the lake to find a more productive spot to fish.

I found a small spring that was flowing into the lake. It was small and bubbled up beneath several chunks of lava and boulders, running about two hundred feet until it poured into the lake.

This was a photographer's paradise with a number of different types of plants and flowers in bloom, a couple of butterflies, and a variety of colors in a backdrop of majestic mountains and trees.

I saw the two fishermen on the opposite side of the lake so I walked around to where they were and took up residence in a small aspen grove flanked by a series of four or five large boulders the size of a pickup truck.

They saw me and walked over to take a break from their endeavors, both sharing their heartfelt discouragement that there must not be any fish in the lake, or if there were, there were very few. Their impatience to make the hike up to Lightning Lake was beginning to show.

The youngest said he had found a "cool" rock that when standing on, the bottom of the lake can be seen. He wanted to take us to it.

With no fish and me looking for more pictures, we climbed back around to where the main creek emptied into the lake. Up the creek and to the side of the hill, a large rock or boulder that looked like a turtle was off to the right. There were several trees and some huckleberry bushes nearby. Berries were picked, and the rock was officially named "Turtle Rock."

Peering down to the lake below, from this vantage point, we could determine the deep and shallow parts of the lake and began talking about where the fish might be. Through the transparent blue water near the center of the lake could be seen two large trees, totally submerged, that looked as though they were still growing. The trees must have been there before the lake was formed—which led us to think that the lake had been formed quickly. Perhaps a lava flow at the far end of the lake created a damming effect so the water backed up to form the lake.

The blues of the water were captivating. There just had to be fish in there! Hope surfaced again by our talking and dreaming.

I had a captive audience; the three of us sat and snacked on granola bars and huckleberries. I took the opportunity to share the story of catching my first fish—a grandfather's prerogative, I suppose.

Reeling in Patience

"When I was little, about three or four years old, I caught my first fish. Mom, Dad, and I were at Red Rock Campground, which was situated on a small clear creek in south central California in the mountains behind Santa Barbara.

"Dad and I were fishing near the downstream tail of a pool with a small riffle at its head. Mom remembered that Dad had cast his line, gave me the pole, and said to be patient and wait—a fish was sure to come along and take the bait. I remember that Dad always used a single salmon egg and completely buried the hook into it so that the fish couldn't see it.

"After a short while, my rod tip started to bounce, and the line drew tight. I had heard both Mom and Dad tell me that to be a good fisherman, you had to be patient. So when Dad said to reel in the fish, I replied, "Not now; I have to be patient. Patience, Dad, patience to be a good fisherman." To that, as the story goes, Mom came over and coached—or more like coaxed—me into reeling in the fish. But my response was still to be patient—so I had to reel it in s-l-o-w-l-y. The fish finally came to shore. My first fish. And then I wanted more. This was the beginning of one of my favorite pastimes.

———————

Patience is a principle that requires one to look ahead and have the vision to anticipate the results. My Dad once said, "Impatience only looks to the here and now, and most often is shortsighted." There is a caveat with patience, however. When the time is right, you have to strike and sometimes strike fast, or the opportunity can be lost. Just like fishing—patience, patience, patience! Then when the fish strikes, you strike back, and the fight is on!

There is also a part of patience that whispers to move to a different spot and try a new tactic. I call that "guided patience." That is where the FIRE Principle again comes into play. Focus on the objective. Gather information. It could be, "There does not appear to be fish here." Look at the resources and engage in action.

Gary, a legendary salmon and steelhead fishing guide on the Siuslaw River in Oregon, once told my brother and I that to catch a salmon or steelhead you have to fish—that means have the bait in the water and pay attention, especially when the "bite is on." One of Gary's pet peeves was not being ready and missing the strike; it was important to be ready at all times. I can still hear him getting on me for missing not one but two strikes within just a few minutes of each other because I was not paying attention. My brother and I used patience, the

FIRE Principle, paid attention to Gary, our information and resource specialist, learned…and always caught fish—big fish.

———————————

Seeing the lake from Turtle Rock set in motion some new ideas of where to try again. A short while later, the three of us were standing where the creek emptied into the lake. Off to the left were the shadows of a deep hole that seemed a likely spot to hold some fish.

I was in my element, camera in hand.

Over the course of the morning, I had taken a number of pictures that framed the guys against the cliffs nearby with the mountain peaks poking up behind and the mirrored water in the foreground. The geologic colors were astounding in this place. It was a wonder that no one else was here. We had been told on our way up that very few people had ever been here, but when we asked why, no reason was given—only that the place had perhaps been forgotten.

"Not much action this morning! Still no luck!" reported the youngest.

His father, I had to hand it to him, was never one to quit; he always was one to keep trying and working to bring results at whatever he did.

The sun was about noon high, and we were getting hungry. The granola bars weren't very satisfying; it was about time for lunch, and stomachs were sharing their cravings.

I heard the comment, "You and Grandpa head back to camp. One or two more casts, and I'll be right up." I had heard that before and had said it many times myself. I knew its meaning: *I'll be up in about an hour.*

Both determined fishermen stayed as I headed back toward camp. On the way I stopped, took a seat on the ground, and rested my head on my jacket near our first stop about fifteen feet up from the rock and branch of the FIRE Principle. A short time later, I awoke to the sounds of commotion in the water a short distance away and saw the third fish pulled from that spot beneath the rock and branch where we were earlier that morning. Three more brook trout were caught in a spot just above the "FIRE hole" as we were now calling it.

The boys were grinning from ear to ear as they held up their catch for pictures.

Once back at camp, I pulled out the pack stove and frying pan. We dined on a nice, simple lunch of fish, dried fruit, and lemonade.

As I lay on my sleeping bag, ready to take another short nap, a voice whispered—"Thanks! I showed Dad the spot and told him what you said about fish and what's important to catch a fish. Like what we have at home—food and a house and stuff—and I added 'family' cuz, well, it's best not to feel lonely. I figured that goes for fish, too! I think that's why we caught enough for lunch. Dad knows about FIRE now and how you and I figured out where the fish were. I remembered the spool of leader you gave me—we used it."

The afternoon was warm. The sun was shining, the lake glistening, and a gentle breeze rustled some leaves. A rather large chipmunk, actually a golden-mantled ground squirrel, about a foot in length, sat just to the right of my sleeping bag and began to chatter.

I looked to the lake and saw father and son having a playful water fight along the shore. I watch as the boys swam out into the lake and headed for an area where there were a series of short cliffs. They pulled themselves up on shore and climbed what looked to be an animal or deer trail up the slope to the top of the cliffs—about fifteen to twenty feet or so high was my best guess. I saw that they had checked to be sure it was a safe place to dive. They jumped off and repeated several times. I was reminded of a time years earlier when I was swimming across a lake with my other sons, the oldest—just him and me, in the Vermont woods, jumping off some cliffs into the cool clear water of a mountain lake. It was as though I were reliving that day—like yesterday, it seemed.

Opportunity, Perseverance, and Determination

The chatter of my small friend brought me back to reality, and I noticed the squirrel had raided the granola bar stash and was dragging a bar along the ground. I didn't have the heart to stop the brazen effort; this was simply making the most of an opportunity, I thought. Cute as it was, when the furry rascal realized that we had food, it could become a pest.

The granola bar dropped to the dirt, and the thief stopped to look at me intently, as if encouraging me to ponder more of life's learning experiences. I imagined the urgent chirps and squeals telling me to not hesitate in recognizing opportunities, to act on them, and to keep at it until success is part of the program. I began to respond with an audible mumble, "You're right, you cute little varmint."

The chatter stopped. The granola bar again firmly in his mouth, the discussion was finished. And we were now short at least one snack.

I pondered for a moment about the priorities of Native Americans in years past and about that story that had been told around the card table during the game night months earlier.

I thought of the chance meeting we'd had with an old Indian in the town where we had stopped for breakfast before our ascent up the narrow dirt road to the trailhead. We had met him while waiting for a table at the town's lone restaurant. We had told him of our intentions and plans to go to Emerald Lake—to which he corrected us that the lake's real name was Thunder Lake.

He began telling a story he said had been told by his father when he was young—just the two of them sitting alongside one of the local creeks. I believe it was the same story my friend had heard that started us on this journey.

The Indian's father had told a story about his own father's success in making it through a legendary winter of cold snow and chilling winds while trying to stay safe from the newcomers who had invaded their lands in the valleys below. They called it the "Legend of Paradise Winter."

But the waitress had interrupted our conversation, and we went to our separate tables.

Following breakfast, we made our way to the general store where, again, the old-timer happened to be. It was here that the boys learned the rest of the story. While I went to fill up the Grand Cherokee with gas, the boys sat on a couple of feed sacks and learned of the Indian family and their flight into the mountains.

The tribal family was forced to climb high into the mountains to escape the pursuit of those who had taken their lands in the valleys below. They were prepared to sacrifice their lives for their culture rather than accept the terms of the reservation. This family had taken their possessions and, wrapped in elk hides, sought to weather the howling wind and freezing storms of winter inside their teepees. They sought to feel secure in the safety of the mountains. Survival or returning to the sacred earth were their only options; they knew the odds most likely favored the latter. They would rather risk death than live on a reservation. Snow piled up and forced them to move to a more sheltered area. They ascended the mountain during a break in the storms, guided by a lone eagle that has since been called the "Eagle of Light," so named by the local tribal elders as a symbol of personal enlightenment and given to those who have survived the winter and difficult times.

They were brought to a place that was sheltered from the winds and storms. The protective cliffs and serrated peaks provided security and protection from their enemies in the valleys below and the fierceness of nature.

Not far below, their winter home was a lake that glistened in the sun reflecting off the ice-encrusted water. It was said that there they resided, perched in their mountain shelter, at the edge of storm clouds. From a vantage point on a cliff above, they could see all of what went on below for as far as an eagle could fly and the sun could shine. The legend said that they found a magical home that winter that saved them and provided them with warmth, protection, shelter, and food.

_____

As I pondered the fabled scenario and story, I visualized the mountains, the snow, and the lake and could almost feel what it must have been like.

As I surveyed my current surroundings with images whirling in my mind, my eyes focused on a depression at the base of a series of cliffs that rose from a small plateau. The depression seemed obscured by some low-growing bushes and three trees—two aspens on the left and one tall spruce on the right. This area was in the general proximity of our newly named "Turtle Rock," though farther up the mountain perhaps three hundred or so yards.

I imagined a camp with a teepee on the small, elevated plateau, and a thin pillar of smoke rising against the rock wall of the home's backdrop. A thought came to mind that if a cave were there, the temperature would be constant, and it could provide them with shelter. I initially dismissed the thought, but as I looked closer, I could see that a cave could very well be there. Was that depression in the cliff a hidden cave? My heart began to beat faster.

I was jolted back to reality by the squirrel's chattering and realized there were now two of them carrying off our snacks for the following day. I had to act; patience was not the order of the moment! The rascals were chased away, but knowing full well that they would now return, we had to be sure to secure all our food after each meal.

We had taken "bear precautions" in the event that a stray bear wandered through camp. We had hoisted all our food packs high off the ground by throwing a rope over a branch of a spruce on the outskirts of the camp, tying the packs to it and pulling it up twelve or more feet in the air. So far, no bear had come through our camp—only ferocious squirrels.

Curiosity had grabbed hold of me, but fatigue had grabbed my body. My mind was racing about the legend, but I was tired. I assume my tiredness was because of the altitude and the fact that I was not in the best of condition for the hiking we had done today and the previous day's packing in. The boys had had to wait for me as we had hiked in, and I was still recovering from that—the fitness of my youth now a memory.

As evening approached, the lake was dimpled with circles from insects being slurped beneath the water's surface. Dinner for sure, we thought. There *were* fish in the lake!

The boys, back from their swim, dried off and changed, were eager to go back to the lake, drawn by the rings in the water that assured fishing success.

My son, with his son, wandered over with fishing rod in hand and asked, "Is there anything we can do to help with dinner?"

I looked at him, looked at the rod, looked back at him, looked at the lake, and said, "It looks like dinner is just waiting for you to bring back to camp." With that, the two of them were off.

I had often done the same with my father. It was Mom who was left to get things ready for our return to camp—sometimes making do with the extra "emergency" dinner she always by "chance" had along. This time I was packing emergency dinners: a couple of packs of Stove Top turkey dressing, eaten by itself or great with any fish that happened to be brought back to camp. I had become quite adept at cooking in foil over an open fire that minimized the use of pots and pans.

The fire was going and most of dinner was ready, but two empty-handed fishermen returned to camp. I motioned them over and pointed to the creek where there were five eight- to ten-inch brook trout lying in the water on a stick.

Lifting them high, the sounds of "Grandpa, where did these come from?" resonated across the campsite.

"Well, I watched you for a few minutes down at the lake and then remembered the nice hole below "Turtle Rock." Well, I guess those fish were destined to be dinner 'cause they just jumped right out of the water and landed on the bank in front of me. I couldn't just leave them there so I brought 'em back to camp."

They both laughed, but I could tell my son was getting a little frustrated. In a few minutes, the fish were wrapped in foil with some celery, bell pepper, onion, a dab of butter, some salt and pepper, and sizzling over a bed of hot coals. We ate the fish and the stuffing, as well as the rest of the reconstituted freeze-dried vegetables. The meal was finished off by sharing an apple cake baked in foil to perfection. I was lucky this time—not one burned spot, preserving my reputation as "King Cook of the Wilderness"—a reputation remembered very infrequently and generally only when dinner turned out right.

Why We Do What We Do

We sat by the evening fire planning the following day's activities: a hike to Lightning Lake—what we had been told was a prime golden trout lake—and checking out the possible cave near Turtle Rock.

The question again surfaced, "Grandpa, why do we do what we do?"

I looked into the inquisitive young eyes to see the intensity of those eyes sincerely searching for understanding.

I had learned over the years that one-on-one times like these are often the best environments to teach or share thoughts, concerns, feelings, and just life in general. Teaching can happen only when those who are taught are ready to hear. You can't really force someone to learn or share their inner feelings and thoughts—just be there and try to recognize the timing.

Sometimes these opportunities just happen; other times, with patience and a little planning, opportunities may surface. That is where doing something together and sharing time comes into play. Cleaning up together earlier in the day had created a time to talk, or exploring, playing a game together, or working on a project. I had learned that the quantity of time was important, not just quality time, to earn trust and develop relationships.

The timing seemed good.

Turning to the young man, I asked, "Remember what we talked about this morning?"

"I remember the FIRE, 'bout getting things done. But I forgot about what makes us do things."

I responded to the "why," reminding him about the match that lights the fire but also told him that it might take a while to really explain in more detail why we do what we do.

To my surprise, a second voice responded, "Dad, why don't you tell us both about that. I think I might like to hear it too."

This was the first time since my son was just a young boy that he had wanted to hear me talk. I had not really had the opportunity to teach many of life's lessons to him. I had wanted to and hoped to, but the unfortunate circumstances, perceptions, and relationship influences of divorce had diverted those attempts. I had missed opportunities. In the following years, I had tried to be patient about creating an environment to be able to just talk to him. I had wanted to be able to help mold my children's values and teach them what I had learned so they wouldn't have to make the same mistakes I had. There were many times I had lost faith that I would ever have any opportunity to do so, but I had worked hard at keeping hope alive for those moments of connection.

This was possibly one of those moments.

With in a few minutes, more wood was on the fire, and the three of us settled down. Now two sets of inquisitive eyes focused on me. I was nervous, hoping that I would be able to take this moment—a moment that I had waited for—and do what I had visualized in my mind many times for more than twenty years.

"Well," I started, "let's bring your Dad up to speed. Do you remember this morning when we were cleaning up? Do you remember what I was saying about important things?"

"Yes," my grandson responded, "About sometimes some things are more important than other things—and different people have different priorities—like doing cleanup or going fishing."

"Yep, that's it," I said as I repositioned my old lucky fishing hat on my head—a hat my father had worn on many of his fishing trips.

"Priorities are what's important, and we have to make decisions about what is most important all the time. And that all depends on what we value and believe."

Values-Beliefs Model

"Something that is unique to the human race is that we make decisions. These decisions are based on what we value and believe. What we value and believe is the foundation for purpose. What happens next is what we do—our behavior. When our values and beliefs are not supported by our behaviors, there is conflict. We cannot continually live in conflict.

I paused. Then said, "We must resolve our conflict to bring our values and beliefs in line with our behaviors or bring our behaviors in line with our values and beliefs. This is how we grow. Growth takes place at different paces and speeds. Sometimes we learn rather quickly; other times it is a more lengthy process filled with a variety of positive and negative influences.

"What we do to resolve our inner conflict is to justify the values and beliefs most important to us, so we either change our behavior to support those values and beliefs, or we justify our behaviors by changing our values and beliefs.

"You can see these two extremes by first considering a drug addict who will sacrifice honesty and integrity to lie and steal to satisfy his need for drugs compared to the person who becomes a religious convert and changes his behaviors to match those values and beliefs that support his newly embraced religious doctrine or testimony.

"Let me show you. I'll try to give you a picture here by the fire."

"Stretching toward the fire, I picked up a six-inch flat rock, and then another more rounded one, and placed them between us on the ground. Motioning toward the stack of firewood, I ask the young men to get three sticks about a foot or so long. Then I created a triangle by placing one stick horizontally between the two rocks and a stick from each rock pointing down to a small piece of a log below.

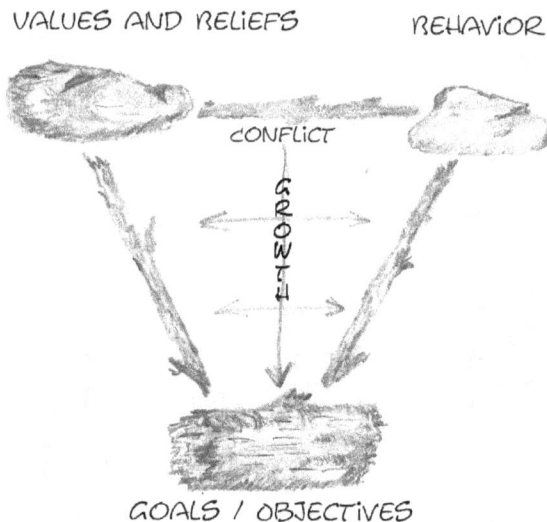

"This flat rock on the left represents what we value and believe. This round rock on the right is what we do—our behaviors. And this piece of wood at the bottom represents a goal or fulfillment of something that we are seeking to achieve. The stick between the "values-beliefs" rock and the "behavior" rock represents conflict. You will notice that to get closer to your goals, the distance between what you value and believe gets closer to behaviors. Conflict reduces the closer you get to the goal.

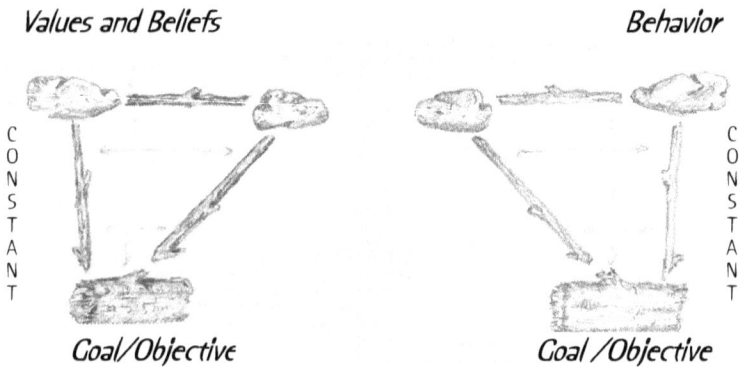

Values and Beliefs   *Behavior*

CONSTANT   CONSTANT

Goal/Objective   *Goal /Objective*

"Now let's do a shift toward a values-beliefs-based model and then let's look at a shift toward a behavior-based model. In the first model on the left, emphasizing values and beliefs, you can see that the values being supported by beliefs remain constant—they don't change. But the behaviors change—the religious convert. And on the right, behavior stays constant, and the values change with the changing beliefs—the drug addict.

"Again, the closer to a goal or objective, the distance between values and beliefs gets closer to behaviors in regard to that particular objective. The result is a reduction of conflict, an increase in growth, and progression closer to the goal. When you reach your goal, values and beliefs are matched with behaviors.

"In actuality, most often we develop our own personal traits based on how we justify and establish our values, beliefs, and behaviors. It is a combination of all components in varying situations and circumstances. This is what determines who we are and what we do—our character. And that is why we do what we do.

"So you see, we do what we do—our behavior—based on what we value and/or believe. The resolution of the differences or conflict between what we value or believe and our actions determine what we do to accomplish the goal. This is growth. Growth is the process of bringing values, beliefs, and behavior in harmony with one another. When we reach this point, we have what could be called goal achievement or fulfillment.

"Think of your life experiences and those people you know or have met. What really brings peace and contentment? What really makes a person happy? And what gives you that feeling of being fulfilled? Have you ever experienced harmony?

"Whether it is winning a championship, closing the big sale, picking the produce from your garden, or giving an anonymous gift—in each case, values and beliefs match behavior. Sometimes during the process of growth, when we are making decisions, we have the experience of feeling good inside about a choice we've made or something we've done, feeling peaceful or having a burst of gladness about what we are doing. This is evidence or confirmation that we are on the right path. We are achieving harmony along the way. We have made the right decision and done the right things that will bring us closer to the bigger objective. It has been my experience that when you live in harmony, most likely you are following your conscience—that little voice inside that seems to guide and direct."

Picking up a stick, the mop top points to the "behavior" rock. The question slips out, "What about those times when I just don't feel comfortable with something or feel that it is wrong? I know that I should follow those promptings and direction, but it's just too difficult. What then?"

"Then you have a decision to make," remarked his father. "Dad, do you mind if I take a stab at this one?"

Pleased, I nodded my head.

"You will have to make a decision about what you value most," he said. "From what Grandpa has said and shown us, it seems you would be in the midst of growth and development. Regardless of what you do, you are making a choice in terms of what you value and believe. Am I on track with that, Dad?"

Grabbing the pot of hot chocolate to refill my cup, I responded, "Absolutely!"

Reaching toward the boys, I refilled their cups and listened with a tender heart as my son continued to counsel his son. "If you choose to continue the behavior or do the thing that you feel uncomfortable about, then you are creating conflict and are actually in the process of changing what you value and believe to justify your behavior. If you choose to not continue with that behavior, then you have identified and have supported those values and beliefs that are most important to you with different behavior."

I then picked up the discussion. "The nugget here is to learn to trust your conscience. It's a gift that's given to every human being. Our conscience is a safety valve and shouldn't be destroyed by inattention. If our conscience is neglected, it gradually becomes less and less sensitive, and we can lose its effectiveness. The flip side is that the more we rely on our conscience, the stronger we become in making decisions that are congruent with our values, and the closer we come to experience the harmony and fulfillment I spoke about before. It seems to me that when you follow your conscience, you become principle centered.

"This is why we do what we do, and this is how to head in the right direction. From beginning to end, our entire life is a process of growth and learning."

The Key to Harmony

"Now there is a key to making this all work—a key that will open doors in one's personal life and career and even bring success to organizations: knowing how to identify and set priorities. And that…will be for another day. That is, if I haven't talked your ears off already." I stirred the fire. "I think that's enough for tonight!"

Both men looked back at me.

"Thanks, Dad." My son then looked skyward and whispered, "I'd like to hear it."

A tear or two welled up in my eyes as I watch the two of them go off together to turn in for the night. To see the two of them together like this filled me with true harmony and well-being. I felt the fulfillment I had talked to them about tonight—that I had done the right thing at the right time. I had followed the small voice within and had the courage to follow through to contribute something at the right time and have it be accepted.

I stayed up, poked the fire, and pondered what had just happened in this momentous night of communication and relationship building. I thought for a moment about this gift and the hope that I had as a father and grandfather that it would continue to manifest itself.

I reflected on the relationship I had with my father. We did things together but didn't counsel very often together, though he was a great example to follow. Later in life, as I began to have more of life's experiences, I learned that seeking his thoughts and perspective became a tremendous resource for me. Unfortunately, that realization occurred too late for us as there were very few of those times left that we could spend together before emphysema took his life.

With those bittersweet feelings of love and regret, I put the fire out, made my way back to my sleeping bag and, once settled in, stared at the stars for a moment, then drifted off to a night full of dreams and visions.

The Legend

Morning came none too soon. All three of us were up just as the birds began to signal the coming day with intermittent chirps and some semblance of song.

"Dad, we don't have to cook anything do we? Can we just get going?" The morning's first words from a teenaged voice.

I had to be honest, I didn't want to cook anything either. Simplicity took priority for food and the day had begun.

Breakfast was granola and some dried fruit. All three of us had awakened several times during the night thinking it was morning. There was an excitement about the coming day. A big event ready to unfold.

The thoughts of exploring my sightings by Turtle Rock were intriguing and garnered excitement of what might be found before we made the ascent to Lightning Lake.

The boys were anticipating their visions of catching fish at Lightning Lake coming true. Though they had not been there, they had heard the stories about the golden trout from a Forest Service worker who came into the general store after the old Indian had left while I was still out getting gas and taking care of repacking. The worker was a timber cruiser, and although he himself had never been there, he told us the old-timer had said the lake was buried into the side of a mountain—perhaps an old crater of sorts and full of fish.

The boys then shared with me more of what the timber cruiser had told them. If the legend were true, the view from the lake would be a photographer's dream. From the southern edge and rim of the lake on a clear day, you could see for several hundred miles across the valleys and lower mountain ranges. The outlet stream from the lake cascaded down the cliffs and disappeared into a lava field below.

Be still my pounding heart! I was excited, adrenalin pumping through my veins. The boys had not told me of the Lightning Lake description. Now, I knew why they were anxious—not only for the fish but also for the adventure.

We had figured it to be a good two- or three-hour hike up to Lightning Lake from our camp. That was at my speed. We would fish for the better part of the day and then make the hike back down. It would be a full day for us, but the anticipated rewards should be worth it—the views, the fishing, and the challenge of making it up and back.

The morning was cooler than normal. Almost cold enough to see our breath, but we knew that the day was going to be warm like it had been all week—especially the previous day.

As we ate breakfast, I shared with the boys my experience of seeing what looked like the description given in the legend. I pointed and described what could be a possible entrance to a cave.

They shared their anxious feelings to get up the mountain, my son saying, "Yeah, that's interesting..." but bargained with me. "How 'bout we take an hour to do a quick exploring job on the way up—but no more than an hour because of the timing for the day?"

I agreed. We had only this one full day left plus the next day to be in camp, clean up, pack up, and head back down the trail to the Jeep.

Gathering up our gear and starting out on the trail, a whoop erupted from the mop top, and a thirteen-year-old's version of "We Are the Champions" ensued. Neither one of us "old folks" joined in, but we did give thumbs up to each other. The boy was excited to get on the trail.

We crossed the creek and within about ten minutes were approaching Turtle Rock.

Standing above Turtle Rock, the sound of an eagle seemed to signal our intention to ascend the rubble toward the cliffs. We stashed our gear between two boulders just to the left side of Turtle Rock. As we looked toward the cliffs, the eagle came into view, soaring effortlessly via the thermals and wind currents. The trail up—looking more like a deer run—was strewn with rocks about the size of footballs.

Scrambling up the rubble leading to the spot I had seen was not an easy task. The easiest path was heading straight for a large evergreen at the top, on the right side of an area that looked to be flat. The two younger men made it to the top in fairly short order. My travel was a different story.

I heard the encouraging words of a grandson, "Hurry up, Grandpa, can't you climb faster?" His father looked at him in a feigned disapproving manner but didn't say anything. He wanted me to hurry up, too.

Once at the top, I again had to rest for a few moments. Climbing up that steep slope of loose rocks was a real test. I was impressed, though. I made it!

"Where's the camera?" asks my son, and at the same time we all realized we had left everything down at Turtle Rock.

A gentle breeze began to rustle the two aspens on the left. The twenty-foot spruce on the right stood vigilant in its protective position near the only pathway up through the rocks to the relatively flat area directly behind the three trees. The area behind the trees was almost semicircular, with about a sixty-foot diameter space in front of the base of the cliffs. The sheer cliffs rose perhaps sixty feet above us. Standing under the aspens and facing the cliffs, my eyes focused on some bushes growing in front of a depression into the face of the cliffs. The overall natural landscape of the area was more typical of an alpine climate, but these bushes seemed out of place—almost tropical with varying shades of green.

"Dad! Grandpa! We should have made our camp up here!" shouted the youngest. "This is a cool place! But I'm ready to go to the lake!" Almost in the same breath while running toward the out-of-place bushes, he continued, "This place right over here looks like a mini-jungle. Look at how big these leaves are!"

Now he began to see that we might be here a little longer than we first planned. The scene before us had captured our interest completely.

Not a lot was said—we just took in our surroundings, observing, minds spinning and whirling like stock cars in a NASCAR race.

Wandering closer, a breeze caught my cheek. It was rather warm as compared to the cool morning we were experiencing so far. As we got nearer to this out-of-place growth, the humid air began to feel as though we were near a waterfall; but there was no evidence of water. We approached "the jungle" as the youngest called it, parted the growth and peered into an opening about ten feet high and about five feet wide. Once inside we found a larger room lit by the sunlight shining through several cracks in the tall, straight walls, and an opening near the top ceiling portion of the room.

Here were not the typical stalactites and stalagmites that one thinks of in a cave. The cave floor was relatively clear and flat. It looked as though some form of wildlife once used it, but there was no recent evidence that we could determine. Further into the cavern, the ceiling was lower. A breeze and the sounds of water were coming up from the back. The temptation to go back into the cavern was strong, but I knew that we needed to have the proper equipment, especially into the darker areas of the cave. Flashlights and ropes would be imperative along with other gear. We determined that safety was our first priority, and we would not put ourselves at risk of an accident.

"Dad, this is incredible! My mind is going a hundred and ninety-two miles an hour! The thoughts of the legend keep racing in my mind. I want to know more about this place and its history!"

We were awestruck!

As we made our way back toward the entrance, the sun shone down on a particular portion of the east wall. This part of the wall was smooth and had pictographs painted on it.

We could recognize the mountains and the lakes quite easily. The larger of the lakes was easily Emerald Lake. In the center of the lake were two trees. We recognized those as the trees we had seen from Turtle Rock. There was a second smaller lake somewhat above the first with what looked to be a sun or sun rays coming from the left side of the lake—a lightning bolt over the right side! Between the two lakes was a teepee. From the teepee to the upper lake and from the teepee to the lower lake was a double line—a pathway apparently—pointing to a turtle drawn at the edge of each lake.

The striking part of the pictograph was that at the center of each lake was a hole the size of a quarter that must have been drilled and then filled with what looked to be gold. On the back of each turtle was another hole that had what looked to be an emerald that fit perfectly.

Also in the pictograph were what looked to be deer and a bear. There were several fish in the lower lake. Mountains surrounded the two lakes, and the teepee with a zigzag line drawn from the teepee to one of the mountains. At the end of that line—which we guessed was another path—were two empty holes similar in diameter to those filled with the gold and about one inch deep.

We were so overcome with fantasy and thoughts of the legend, and how this must be evidence that the legend was true…time had escaped us.

It was now past noon, and we would not be able to make the hike to Lightning Lake. Hungry now, we decided to get the camera, go back to camp for some lunch, grab the topographical map, try to take a closer look at the surrounding area, and return to the plateau.

The fact that we were not going to make it to Lightning Lake didn't bother us until my son began describing the lake the way the old Indian and the timber cruiser had. What we were actually seeing fit into the legend and the description of Lightning Lake; we were thinking now that the legend was true. The old Indian's presence seemed to be becoming more and more significant.

Back at camp, we refueled with a late lunch, and with our limited resources we were ready to venture back up the rubble. We knew we needed more gear and information before we could really explore in depth. But there was more than enough to take in, contemplate, and check out.

Curiosity got the better of us. Looking back at the site from where we were sitting, we had a better view. We unfolded the trail map, opened the topographical map, and discovered that Lightning Lake was almost directly over where we had been standing at the site. There were a series of cliffs, one above the other, on the side of the mountain. We could see from our camp that there was a lava field at the base of the upper cliffs and figured Lightning Lake was on top of those. A steep mountain continued to rise behind that. From our vantage point, though we couldn't see clearly, it appeared that the lake was situated on the side of that mountain according to the topographical map.

We spent the remainder of the day carefully looking for more evidence of the legend and making side excursions away from the "Legend Camp" as we named it.

Then, as the afternoon began to turn toward evening, came the simplest and most intriguing of questions: "Grandpa, why did we find this place and no one else has found it?"

I paused for several moments. Thought. And with a paused response said, "I don't have an answer. I just don't know." None of us could answer. The "why" became the prominent topic of our evening discussion. "Why us?" and "why was this place unknown?"

"We have got to come back here!" exclaimed my son, excitement in his voice. More questions voiced by all of us and no real answers—just speculation. We tried to conceal the location of the cave entrance and cover any evidence of our arrival. Then back to camp.

We made dinner, ate, and talked about our newfound discovery. The conversation turned to what it must have been like, for those people who had made it through the winter in that paradise of a cave...We wondered what they did and where they went after that winter. Our questions turned to the previous day's discussion about priorities and what must have been important to them. I thought about the pictographs and why they put them on the walls. According to the old Indian, that family's priorities apparently were family, their traditions, and the preservation of their culture.

We could create a story with the lake, the fish, animals, the fire, the lake above with the sun, and the lightning bolt. Although we couldn't figure it all out, piecing it together was fun and captured our enthusiasm. From the wall paintings in the cave, we learned about the lakes, food, and the sun. We surmised that the cave had provided them shelter, the spring provided water, and the lake provided fish for food. Still, we could not put it all together—what did the sun represent? The emeralds, the gold, and some of the other etchings? For now we could go no farther.

As we discussed the events of the day and how this all came about, we discovered that we had used and were using the FIRE Principle. This had become a real-life workshop. We needed more information and more resources before we could really engage in a workable plan. And what was our real objective?

The youngest went off to sleep, no doubt full of thoughts and dreams from our day of adventure. The thoughts of returning for another trip spun in our adult minds as well. We were going to return, but the real question was when? With work and other commitments, how soon could we get back?

Decisions

In the quiet of the evening with the two of us now, my son turned to me with a more serious look and said, "Dad, I need to talk…I have a real important decision that I'm making, and I need your advice. I know that I've never asked for it before, but I am asking you now. Thinking about the people who found that cave, I believe they had some very important decisions to make: whether to stay up here for the winter and risk the effects of the snows and cold or to come down to the valley below and risk danger from the settlers who had chased them from their original home…or conform to the new life and acceptance of living on a reservation.

"I feel like I'm faced with similar decisions, only in the corporate world. That world can be life altering in terms of expectations and how it influences the development of one's personal values and beliefs. Our personal values and beliefs can be compromised, or they can be strengthened through choices and decisions. Those decisions depend on what our priorities are—what a person truly values and believes, and our true character is defined by the decisions we make and the actions that follow. In the case of the Indian family, their values and beliefs are very evident."

I was quiet—not wanting to interrupt his train of thought.

"I've been offered a promotion with my company," he stammered, "and at the same time, I have been asked by another competing company to interview with them. Both jobs will pay considerably more money than I am now making. Each will give me more responsibility and a higher profile and visibility. If I stay with my current employer, I will have to move again. If I get the competitor's job, I will stay but will have to move later to get the next promotion. My three kids are getting to the point where I'm not sure if moving is the best thing for them. My wife would really like to stay home and not have to work, but our bills tell us that she has to keep working outside the home, so money is a factor. If I work more hours, I won't be able to spend time with the kids and share their growing years—not that I spend a lot of time with them now, but I would like to. I've already been gone a lot, and I've bought extra things on credit to try to make up for my not being home. This has put more financial strain on us.

"To top it all off, about three weeks ago, I got a call from an old college buddy. We've talked off and on about doing some kind of business together but never seriously. He suggested that the time might be right to actually do something instead of just talk.

"So I have a lot of things to consider! You've been talking about priorities and why we do what we do. I guess here's another real-life case study for you, right, Dad?"

"Well…" I paused for a moment, picked up a small thin stick and began peeling the bark. I thought about how I had prepared for this moment and about what Stephen Covey said, "Seek first to understand, then to be understood." Now was not the moment for me to offer the counsel he sought from me. Now was time to listen; I really wanted to understand. My heart was opening.

I continued, "There is a Cheyenne proverb that says something about walking a mile or a couple of moons in the other's moccasins. I think part of that means that we have to try to understand each other. Can you tell more of your thoughts?" I remained quiet, pondering the situation and wondering what was next.

My son continued, "I never did say much growing up because I was always afraid that I wouldn't say the right thing or someone else would get upset because of what I thought, and I didn't want to hurt your feelings. There were some things that happened to us when we were kids that were hard, and I didn't think that you cared. As I got older, I guess I thought you did care about me, but I was afraid to risk the hurt of finding out maybe you didn't…" He paused.

I then spoke, deliberately and slowly, "Let me ask you this: Do you trust me now? Do you believe I care now?"

"Yes I do, or I wouldn't have asked you about this situation," he responded. "You talked about information and resources, and I think it's about time I use what's been right in front of me—you."

With a slight quiver in my voice, the words slowly trickled out, "As you got older...I remember letting you know that I would offer my counsel and what I thought, but that you should make your own decisions and I would be supportive."

All I wanted to do was listen now. I had never experienced this kind of honesty with him—or with anyone else for that matter.

Lifting his head with an expression of relief, he said, "Well, it's about time I took it to heart and listened to what you have to say and then make a decision. I heard you talk about the FIRE Principle, that our values and beliefs control our behavior and some of the other things...and think I need some help—that would be the information and resources needs from the FIRE Principle, wouldn't it? So what do you think about this situation?"

Looking up from my half-peeled stick and pointing toward the stream, I asked, "Do you remember, about lunch time, the other day you caught those fish out of that hole right over there?"

"Yes...and I was told why there would be fish there. I did what my son told me and bang! The fish hit it, and we had lunch. I think that's what started me thinking a little more about what I had missed over the years. Sharing more experiences with you and learning from your experiences."

Continuing to peel my stick, "So, what did the boy tell you?"

"He told me about basic needs—and to think like a fish. I take that to mean that I need to put myself in the others' shoes to understand what their motives and objectives are."

"That's how I see it, too! Remember the rocks that I set out by the fire the other night?" I began to scratch out a triangle in the dirt with my stick.

He nodded.

"Those rocks and twigs are a model of why we do what we do. When values and beliefs support our behavior and our behavior supports our values and beliefs, there is harmony or fulfillment—real goal or vision achievement. Those are the times when you feel that calm, peaceful, positive, confident feeling inside—that is an indicator of principle-centered growth.

"Problems occur when our behaviors, or even our environment, influence us to justify and change those things that are most important to us—our real priorities. Then we are back into conflict, and we risk justifying our behavior by changing core values and beliefs.

"The other night we didn't finish, but there was something else that I wanted to share about priorities, and you said that you would like to hear it. Now I think it's time to share that. It's a priority or decision-making tool. Are you up for that now?"

"Yes! I'd like to hear it."

The Priority Assistant

"Many years ago, on a business trip, I was walking along the bank of the Yakima River in Yakima, Washington. I was a sales rep in the telecommunications industry selling long distance and data services at the time. I thought about how to help my customers prioritize things that had to do with the services I had to offer. I was thinking to myself, "There has got to be something different—a way to figure things out to determine what is most important." The thought of a tool came to mind. I remembered that years earlier, I'd had a professor in college who taught about decision making. So I'm going to share with you a tool that came to mind there on the banks of the Yakima River—a way to help you prioritize what's important to you. I call it the "Priority Assistant" because it assists in making decisions with a visionary perspective of establishing priorities.

"It is not perfect, but it can be very helpful—sort of like Ben Franklin's Pros and Cons list.[4] Simply put: Franklin drew a line down the middle of the page. The topic was put at the top and then the reasons against, or No's, on the left and reasons for, or Yes's, on the right. Count them up and the column with the number of the most important items wins. Of course, Ben explained it in more detail than this, but the general idea was to take time and have a method to evaluate and think things through.

"Here...I have a piece of paper left in my notepad; it might be better to visualize the Priority Assistant. Let me draw a matrix.

"Now, what are the criteria that you are considering in making your decision? For example, if you say 'recognition,' in a work environment, recognition might be a promotion, winning a major sales contest, or having management acknowledge your efforts with less micromanagement. So 'recognition' is your personal definition. Just be specific and consistent in defining the elements."

With some hesitation and effort, he identified five elements important to his pending decision as related to career and family priorities: money, personal time, home location, career recognition, and family time.

I continued, "Being able to identify and define what your considerations are is the key factor of the Priority Assistant."

After several minutes of discussion and some thoughtful effort, and in a tone reflecting a confident, young executive, he arrived at a concise list defining his considerations.

"OK, Dad, 'money' means finances and income as it relates to our bottom line; 'personal interest' has to do with my personal time, like hobbies or what I do outside of family and work; 'home' has to do with the location of home and how that relates to the stability of our family environment; 'career recognition' means a promotion or a move with increased responsibility; and 'family time' means time developing meaningful relationships with my wife and children."

With a nod and a proud fatherly smile, I said, "Let's put these into the matrix and see where you stand. Let's see what might be most important. "The X's are pairings that we can disregard because they are duplicates."

Here is the first part of what we wrote:

PRIORITIES	PERSONAL INTEREST	MONEY	CAREER RECOGNITION	HOME	FAMILY Relations
PERSONAL INTEREST	X				
MONEY	X	X			
CAREER RECOGNITION	X	X	X		
HOME	X	X	X	X	
FAMILY Relations	X	X	X	X	X

I handed the piece of paper and pen to him and ask, "So what's most important as we defined these issues? Write your answer in the appropriate box." We addressed each element working across each row.

"Personal interest or money?" I asked. "Personal interest or career? Personal interest or home? Personal interest or family time?"

"Now, we'll go to the second row. Money or career? Money or home? Money or family time?"

"Now, career or home? Career or family time? Home or family time?"

"Now count the total number of entries or responses for each element. Go ahead and fill in the number for each one of them."

"So the one with the most entries is most likely what is most important?" he asked.

"Yes, and the next most is second, and so on. You now have a ranking as to your priorities. Go ahead and write the number "1" by the one that came out on top and number "2" for the next one and so on. And, as I said before, it may not be completely scientific, but it gives you an idea of where you stand and what your priorities are."

Pointing to the number one–ranked priority and with a sense of excitement in his voice, he enthusiastically blurted, "Dad, this is amazing! It didn't come out anything like I thought it would. I'd been really believing that what's now my number three was number one. I think that I might be in the midst of a paradigm shift here."*

"Well," I said, "now you've just experienced the Prioirity Assistant. You don't have to use it, but it's a tool that I've found helpful when making important decisions. Even buying a car or purchasing a house, making family decisions or business decisions—it seems to work; at the very least, it will assist in the process of identifying possibilities.

"Let me just take a minute and share a little more about it. Here is a Priority Assistant I left in my notebook for purchasing a car. As it turns out here, gas mileage was the most important. But it will be different for each person because what each person values is different.

CAR	Initial Cost	Maint Cost	Gas mileage	Model (style)	Color	TOTAL
Initial Cost	X	IC	GAS	IC	IC	3
Maint Cost	X	X	GAS	Mod	MC	1
Gas mileage	X	✓	X	GAS	GAS	4
Model (style)	X	✓	X	✓	Mod	2
Color	X	X	✓	X	X	0

"The Priority Assistant can also be used to set daily, weekly, annual, or life time priorities. It is pretty dynamic.

Organizational Priority Assistant

Picking up my stick again and peeling the last piece of bark, I included with great thought, "Even in making corporate or organizational decisions, if you work through the Priority Assistant as a team or a committee, it will foster discussion and open doors of communication as to what is really valued and what the collective priorities are. Does that help at all?"

Still looking at his Priority Assistant, my son replied, "I think it does. I think I can see where I need to be and how I need to focus my energies. I can also see us as a family, taking some family time one evening and doing the Priority Assistant together. This will bring us all onto the same page so that we'll all be aware of what we are doing and why.

"Your comment about daily, weekly and annual priorities is also a good point. How often do we flutter around trying to figure out what should be done first or what the priorities are for the week or for the year. This can help bring into perspective how a short term priority might contribute to an annual goal. Doing something in the short term might hold a different priority for the first 3 months than it would towards the end of the year. So some priorities might change given the nature of the goal or objective associated with it.

"In my work group, I can see several applications—that is, if I'm going to stay at my current position. I can see that it will also take some facilitation skills to keep everyone on track, but I think I can do that. I think there are times where it might be appropriate to call in a neutral facilitator to conduct a Priority Assistant session in a corporate setting.

"You know, Dad, I'm actually feeling inside what you talked about a while ago—a peaceful, calm feeling, and a feeling of determination to become actively engaged—the feelings of doing the right thing. I am feeling quite confident and excited about the direction I should follow.

"This has helped establish in my mind the relationship my career has with my family and personal interests in terms of my priorities. I really do want what I value and believe to match what I do."

Stay the Course

Then I asked him, "As your Dad, can I just say one last thing with regard to success in decision making?"

"Sure."

I put my stick down, put my elbows on my knees, and clasped my hands together. "My father gave me this counsel a long time ago when I was quite young, and I have never forgotten it."

I turned to him and looked him straight in the eyes, just as my father had looked into mine, and said, "Once you make a decision and you feel the peace of conscience that it is the right decision, see it through. Don't stop. It *will* be the right thing for you. Stay the course!"

I unfolded my hands and straightened up. "A minute ago you referred to determination. I call it 'resolute determination.' Abraham Lincoln said, 'You cannot fail if you resolutely determine that you will not.[5]'"

"It's having the quiet resolve of confidence and trust to engage in a course of action and keep moving—even if you have to review the plan and make adjustments—it's easier to steer a moving bicycle than one that is stationary. Don't stop. Momentum is created when you have an idea and begin to pedal. There is more energy expended when you first begin something than at any other time. That momentum is propelled by a charge of optimism and enthusiasm that power the take-off.

"It's also true that your vision will expand; you will visualize more and increase your experience base in regard to your objective once you are moving. Experience in and of itself can provide insight to solidify or assist in accomplishing your vision and goals."

We were both oblivious to the shooting stars overhead. The night had wrapped its arms around us. The crispness and clarity of the night had given pause to consider the awakening that had occurred and what the future might hold.

Harmony Revisited

Three sleeping bags were motionless throughout the night. Exhaustion seemed to have overtaken all of us. Or was it contentment and peace? Perhaps it was the harmony that was discovered amid the mountains and lakes high above, away from the drones of the city.

As the stars faded, I awoke early as usual and noticed that the other two sleeping bags were empty. Looking into the dim morning light down by the lake, two figures could be seen making their way toward the shore near where the outlet stream escaped the serene morning water.

Putting on my boots, I said a prayer of thanks. "Heavenly Father, thank you for giving us these moments." And then a brief request: "Heavenly Father, would it be possible for us to catch some fish this morning?"

The feelings of peace and contentment embraced the morning air. We were doing the right things. We were sharing an experience that can only be described within one's heart and soul. I knew that all three of us had felt the internal awakening and sense of gratitude that accompanies fulfillment and harmony.

I do know this: that it is each person's responsibility to learn to recognize these feelings of peace and contentment as a guide and direction in making decisions. And only experience can teach us to develop trust in the internal promptings and feelings we have and receive. Only experience can teach that.

The water dimpled—fish rising on the smooth, glass surface. The ripple of each rise traveled effortlessly and then disappeared into the liquid mirror.

Clamoring over a boulder and coming into their view, the boys' heads turned, and all three of us exchanged smiles.

"Dad, you're up a little late," quips my son.

His tease is accepted.

"Son, what would you suggest I fish with this morning?

"Well, I applied a little FIRE." he responded. "I took some time and looked closely in the water. I found this little small bug larvae just under the surface of the water, so I thought I'd try something that looked pretty similar. I think this is a Renegade, a number 14, or maybe it's that old thing you gave me years ago that I've never used. It looks close to what was in the water."

With a grin and motioning over to the mop top, he teases, "The 'kid' is going to try a small, little brass lure to see if the flashing metal blades will bring a strike.

"So it's your choice. Let's get some different things going, create some information and resource material, execute an action plan, and reevaluate if we need to until we catch fish. What do you think?" he said, shrugging his shoulders playfully.

Pausing and then in my slow morning voice, "By the way...that 'old thing' is called a Royal Wulff, and you might also try that Elk Hair Caddis. I think I'm going to use a single salmon egg though. I like the idea of trying different things to see what works."

There was always a small jar of salmon eggs in the bottom of my fishing bag. I always had a jar, but I had not actually used any for years and years. Each, and I suppose it's a ritual by now, I go down to a tackle shop and buy a new bottle of eggs—always ready to use them as my father had. At one time, I had become a fly-fishing purist but not anymore. Today, it just seemed like the right time to use a salmon egg—most likely because of the thoughts I'd had of yesteryear when I was with my father and mother fishing by Red Rock. Nostalgia. The feelings of that moment. A memory...a cherished memory.

We exchanged a few more fishing tips, and the rod action began to heat up.

As the sun rose over the mountaintops, the motionless, glassy water released the golden colors that had flashed beneath its surface into a flurry of airborne activity. The fish slapped back into the water only to reemerge and repeat the acrobatics. Success hit the Renegade first. After the second fish on the Renegade, the two of us with spinning rods switched over to a clear plastic bubble filled about half full of water and a fly. I put on a Royal Wulff, and the mop top grabbed the other Renegade. Soon all three rod tips were bent by fish being caught and many more goldens caught and released by the three of us.

This time pictures were taken.

We had thought the golden trout were only in the upper lakes. We hadn't realized that there were goldens right here in Emerald Lake! Of course, from our previous day's efforts, there was no way of really knowing there was much of anything in that lake.

By mid morning, hunger drove us back to camp. Nine fish were kept for breakfast—three each, all about eleven or twelve inches long. These were big for native goldens.

"Grandpa, these golden trout are the best fish I have ever eaten!"

"That's because they're as good as gold!!" I continued to tease, "And if you cook them to a golden brown, then there you have it—perfection. Just don't be fooled by the 'fool's golden trout. If you ever catch one of them, be sure to let it go; they taste terrible no matter how you cook them because they are not really trout at all—fake trout!"

"You can't fool me any more; I'll FIRE you! I know how to figure things out. And if you're not careful, I'll figure you out too, Grandpa! You're talking about the sucker fish, and you're not going to make a sucker out of me!"

We all laughed and enjoyed the moment.

Then my son said pensively, "To change the subject...Dad, can I tell you a secret?"

"Sure."

"I've always wanted to catch fish like you. But I only occasionally really catch fish. It's sort of irritated me in the past." He continued, "I remember going fishing once with my friend, Mark. He was getting up in age, in his late eighties, and I think he really just needed someone to make sure he stayed on the road when he drove his truck and boat up the mountain. He loved to fish.

"That day we enjoyed storytelling, and I enjoyed hearing his stories of life and his attitude toward making a successful life. On the way home, he asked me about the day. I responded that we didn't catch many fish, so I guess it wasn't as successful as it could have been.

He turned and said, "I think we had a great day fishing. It's just the catching wasn't so good."

"Dad, the last few days have been some of the best days I've had. The fishing was exceptional and the catching—though I have to admit I was a little impatient in the beginning—the catching was great. Most important was not the fish; it was the time we were able to share. As my friend

Mark taught me that day, we are each responsible for how successful we are. The attitude that we approach life with can really make a difference. "So, Dad, it is true: 'It ain't gotta be the way it's always been.' We do have the ability to change—anything, that is, if we recognize the need to set priorities and act according to what we truly value and believe."

Head for Home

We were packed; the camp was cleaned up. There was very little evidence that we had been there. During the downhill trek back to the Jeep, thoughts and chatter revolved around the mystery that we had uncovered. Why was this place seemingly unknown? What about the emeralds, the gold, and how did that tribe or family survive the winter? What was the meaning of the writings on the wall? Questions kept coming, rapid-fire, to all three of us. The questions that captured our interest most were these: "Whatever happened to them?" "Did they continue to live there?" "If not, where did they go?" There was simply no evidence of what happened to them. Perhaps that is what makes it a legend—with more questions to ask back in town.

We decided to keep Emerald Lake a secret, at least for now. Over the course of the next few months, we would make plans to come back to the lake and to search out the "Legend of Indian Winter Paradise."

Once we had the Jeep loaded and were heading back to the small outpost of a town, the young mop top thoughtfully grabbed my sleeve, looked over at me, and said, "Grandpa, thank you for bringing us up here and having this trip! It was more than just a fishing trip!"

His voice was not that of a high-energy young teen but that of a young man who had begun the journey of a lifetime. There was a different quality to his voice—a sincerity that penetrated the way he spoke to his grandfather. There were unspoken feelings of gratitude. No additional words were necessary—only communication from deep within.

"You're welcome," I replied. "Thank you for coming. It was a wonderful trip, a memory—something that can never be taken away. And now I have something to tell you and your Dad.

"Remember when I told you about catching fish down by the "FIRE hole," that there were some things everyone needs, things like food and shelter? Well, there is one more thing that we all really need that is a critical component to each person's character and sometimes we really miss."

"What's that Grandpa?"

"That is the need to be loved and appreciated. Do you know that I love you, your father, and your whole family?"

There was a moment of silence, but the feelings among us were too full for the confines of the vehicle.

Sometimes there are those special moments, moments that you cannot predict and that words cannot describe. The question is, "Are we able to recognize them and grasp their impact?"

These moments occur not only in a family or personal relationship setting but also in a business or work environment. We all need the assurance of value, and we all respond to appreciation when it is genuinely and sincerely given.

My grandson responded, "Yeah, I know, sometimes I don't show it like I should, but I know."

We had decided not to stop in town but to head straight for home—sort of like cows heading for the barn at feeding time; there's just no stopping them. Plus the commitments and schedules that were part of our busy lives awaited our arrival back at home. We knew that if we stopped in town, we would not want to leave for a long time, and we might create unwanted interest in what we had discovered.

Out of the mountains, driving through that rustic weathered town, there, sitting under an old gnarled oak tree beside the road was the old Indian. His hat was off and his long, braided, gray hair draped on his shoulders. As we drove past, his head followed our car. His right hand then rose up about belt high and opened into a slow wave—as if he knew something we didn't.

My son turned to me and, in a defining moment, with purpose in his voice, softly said, "Dad, there is more to living life than just stories. Life is about making good decisions, developing a sound personal character, and defining the real personal purpose that drives our life."

At that same moment, out of the corner of my eye, I caught a glimpse of an eagle circling in the updrafts high above. This symbol of the "Eagle of Light" sent goose bumps down my back.

There has got to be more, not only to this legend but also the feelings of purpose, fulfillment, and harmony that had been experienced by all of us; there just has to be. For me, I am determined for us to continue the course that has been set.

END

* Reader: Now that you've read the story, go back to the Priority Assistant on page 80 and work through it yourself. You will determine what the son's decision will be.

Use the Priority Assistant on the next page . Go ahead and fill it in (use pencil).

For more information and help "Decisionary Leadership: Tools for Growth" has been developed as a resource and guide to help with all of the Ain't Gotta Be (AGB) Tools.

Priority Assistant

Personal Priorities	Personal Interests	Money	Career Recognition	Home	Family Relationships	TOTAL	Rank
Personal Interests	X						
Money	X	X					
Career Recognition	X	X	X				
Home	X	X	X	X			
Family Relationships	X	X	X	X	X		

Factors

Be specific and detailed in the definition of each term or factor.
Change the factors to suit individual options if needed

Use the blank Priority Assistant to evaluate other decisions and priorities.

Priority Assistant

TITLE	A	B	C	D	E	TOTAL	Rank
A	X						
B	X	X					
C	X	X	X				
D	X	X	X	X			
E	X	X	X	X	X		

Factors

Be specific and detailed in the definition of each term or factor.

Below is a graphic representation for understanding the Values-Beliefs Model and how the components of the model actively contribute to goal achievement.

Goal and Growth Motivation
Values Beliefs Model

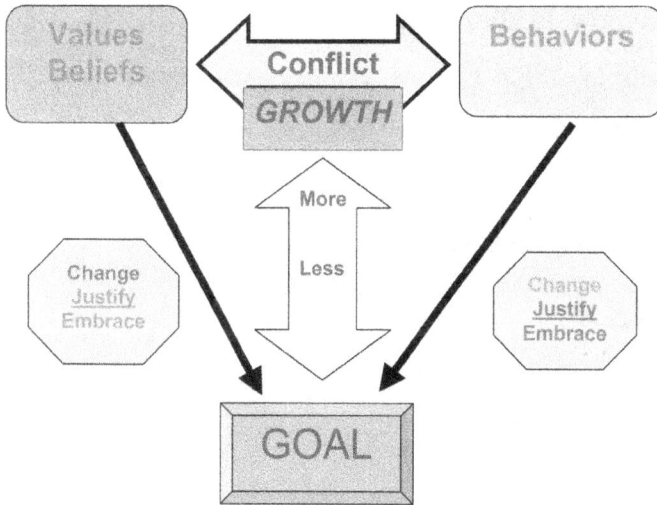

Values Beliefs

Conflict

GROWTH

Behaviors

More

Less

Change
Justify
Embrace

Change
Justify
Embrace

GOAL

.

Decisionary Leadership:
Tools for Growth

The guide to implementing the "Ain't Gotta Be" tools.

A complete description, explanation, and guide for the Values-Beliefs Model, the FIRE Principle, the Priority Assistant, and other helps can be found in the "Ain't Gotta Be" guide **Dicisionary Leadership: Tools for Growth**. Also included are templates for various Priority Assistant topics, such as choosing where to go on vacation, setting money priorities, real estate, determining the most important political issues, and creating your own Priority Assistant.

For more information

www.aintgottabe.com

To order Decisionary Leaership:Tools for Growth

go to

www.decisionary.com

Notes

[1] Victor Frankl, *Man's Search for Meaning* (Boston, Massachusetts: Beacon Press, 1992), XX.

[2] Stephen Covey, *The 8th Habit* (New York: Free Press, 2004), XX.

[3] Ibid., 162.

[4] Ben Franklin, Letter to Joseph Priestley (London. September 19, 1772); "Letter to Joseph Priestley," in *Benjamin Franklin Sampler* (New York: Fawcett, 1956), XX.

[5] A. Lincoln, Letter to George Latham, July 22, 1860
http://www.thelincolnlog.org/view/1860/7/22
Basler, Roy P., Marion Dolores Pratt, and Lloyd A. Dunlap, eds., *The Collected Works of Abraham Lincoln*,Vol 4:87. Springfield, IL: Abraham Lincoln Association; New Brunswick, NJ: Rutgers University Press, 1953.

Acknowledgements

I would like to pay tribute to all those who have been a part of this project coming together. From those that I met on airplanes and dropped in to see in offices, to my friends, customers, family members, and coworkers that read, gave feedback, and responses throughout all stages of putting ink on paper.

I would like to recognize those neighbors and friends that came to my home that first evening to listen to the concepts and principles, see what I was doing, let me know if it made sense, and then gave feedback and asked questions: Laura Dalton, for continuous encouragement and organizing the "Lincoln City Retreat" and those that participated; Erin Robison, who gave me the initial chance to present Decisionary Leadership several times in work groups. All of these opportunities, and others not mentioned, helped to hone the presentation into what is contained on these pages.

I would like to especially thank my wife, Lynn, for her patience and encouragement, through all the starts and stops, to keep at it for all the years it took to finally get it completed. My brother, Rhio O'Connor, who defied the odds in his fight with mesothelioma and lived 7½ years longer than anyone thought. Whose encouragement, thoughts, inspiration, dedication, and belief in me and in what he was doing, and did, have been an inspiration and example not only to me but thousands of others. To David Bird for encouragement and guidance in the early stages of book development, and Eva Long, my editor, for her enthusiasm and expertise in bringing this project to final fruition.

The following list is not complete by any means but are some of those who I wanted to be sure are recognized for being the motivation to persevere and finish this project:

My family: My father and mother, James O'Connor and Rheo O'Connor; Lynn O'Connor, my wife; Sheryl (Alan) Fox, my sister; Rhio (Arlene) O'Connor, my brother.

My Children: JT, Emily (Sean), Anya (Randy), Abram (Tracy), Kris, Katie (Eric), Anna (Bram), Sam, Mary, and family addition Wendy.

Grandchildren: Felicity, Kylie, Troy, Zachary, Isabelle, Joshua, Jeremy, Luke, Jacob, Courtney, Todd, Sage, Awen, Sonya, and more to come...

This project has been a testament to me of the fact that there is a divine source of enlightenment, peace, and fulfillment and that there is a Heavenly Father who loves and cares for each of us.

About the Author

Robert Lee Houtz O'Connor

Robert started life in Solvang, California, and grew up in Santa Maria, California. After receiving his, affectionately called, "fourteen-year Bachelor's degree" from Brigham Young University in psychology and a minor in communications in 1987, he developed a career in sales beginning in the food industry and then moved to telecommunications and on to pharmaceuticals. With an entrepreneurial heart, he is a promoter and proponent of home-based business development and currently considers himself a "regular guy" who works out of his home.

Having lived in Oregon since 1990, Robert has taken advantage of the outdoors and has enjoyed the many aspects of outdoor life and sports that he was taught to appreciate as a youth: from camping and fishing to photography; from following the local sports teams to youth involvement with the Boy Scouts of America and church organizations.

Ain't Gotta Be the Way It's Always Been was written initially as a tool to try to communicate to my children and grandchildren some concepts, principles, and values that have been part of my life. The story is fictitious, with elements of history from the relationships and experiences that I have had throughout my life with family, friends, and acquaintances. The values, beliefs, concepts, and counsel given in the story are based on what I believe to be truth. Many of the events described in the story actually happened. Some of the events I wish had happened. And others are just made up parts of the story.

The Priority Assistant was initially put on paper during a walk along the Yakima River contemplating how to increase sales by assisting customers in making decisions. I had recalled a segment in one of my college courses where the professor had talked about creative decision-making ideas and methods. Sitting by the side of the river, I sketched out a decision-making matrix based on what I could remember from that class.

I began using the matrix on occasions in the early 1990s as a sales aid to assist customers in setting priorities in regard to telecommunication and data decisions. It morphed into a personal, everyday, and business decision-making aid. It has since been used in helping individuals set personal life course priorities and in various counseling circumstances, as well as purchasing furniture and cars, deciding where to go on vacations, and even establishing political priorities during elections.

The Values-Beliefs Model was an inspiration one evening in the mid-1990s when staying late after work contemplating why a family member made certain decisions and choices that were not congruent with past established values and beliefs. Over the years of evaluation and application, it has proved a valuable tool in counseling and understanding behavior, values, and beliefs—elements that guide a person to embrace the character traits that build identity.

The FIRE Principle surfaced while writing "Ain't Gotta Be" as a metaphor that could have been taught and has since been taught in a variety of circumstances.

What about Hope?

Where there is no hope, there is no reward, and the feelings of charity and love will dwindle and die...so I have learned to keep trying, to have faith, and not give up hope. By working in faith and maintaining hope, I have come to experience the sweetness of fruition, on occasion, when trust is exhibited and love abounds. We were put on this earth to laugh, play, and experience joy while working diligently to reach our full potential!

- Ain't Gotta Be the Way It's Always Been

www.ingramcontent.com/pod-product-compliance
Lightning Source LLC
Chambersburg PA
CBHW070526030426
42337CB00016B/2122